ROGER BOULTON

SOUTHWESTERN ONTARIO

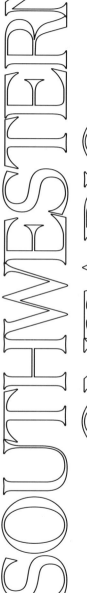

STEWART
HOUSE

Southwestern Ontario has some of Canada's finest farmland.

Published in Canada in 1990 by Stewart House
481 University Avenue
Toronto, Ontario
M5G 2E9

(previous page) Aerial view of Elora with the Grand River and
the Elora Mill.

Canadian Cataloguing in Publication Data

Boulton, Roger
  Southwestern Ontario

(Canadian places series)
ISBN 1-895246-00-8

1. Ontario – Description and travel – 1981–
– Guide-books* 2. Ontario – Description and
travel – 1981–   – Views.* 3. Erie, Lake,
Region – Description and travel – Guide-books.*
4. Huron, Lake, Region (Mich. and Ont.) –
Description and travel – Guide-books. 5. Erie, Lake,
Region – Description and travel – Views. 6. Huron,
Lake, Region (Mich. and Ont.) – Description and
travel – Views. I. Title. II.Series.

FC3095.S68A3 1990   917.13'2044   C90-094385-8
F1059.S68B6 1990

Produced by Boulton Publishing Services Inc., Toronto
Printed and bound in Hong Kong by Book Art Inc., Toronto

Southwestern Ontario, beautiful, peaceable, infinitely rich in the intimate association of people with the land, quietly accepting the passage of history and the passing on of traditions from generation to generation. First cleared by the French in the early eighteenth century, then more extensively settled by the Loyalists, including the Mohawks, the region has since become home to immigrants from England, Ireland and Scotland, from Pennsylvania's Mennonite community, from Germany and now from around the world. Before emancipation came in the United States more than 25,000 slaves fled here to find freedom. All these many diverse peoples form a harmonious and quintessentially Canadian mosaic. Fine cities grew up, some of the most gracious in North America. Great universities also. Some of the most fertile farms in Canada have remained under luxuriant cultivation and the countryside has been largely spared the degradations of urban sprawl that have blighted first-class land elsewhere. Here in this

The 'Kissing Bridge' at West Montrose, last of Ontario's covered bridges, was built in 1881 and stretches 197 feet across the Grand River.

Aerial views of Guelph.

book are the mansions and farmhouses, festivals and fairs, chapels and cathedrals, college campuses, art galleries, museums, historic sites and classical architecture, the streets of Elora, Guelph, Kitchener, Waterloo, Stratford and Goderich, Sarnia and Windsor, Dresden and Brantford, Port Stanley, Port Burwell, Port Dover and so on all around. Southwestern Ontario is one of the last most traditionally Canadian Places, quiet achievement of a vision for a better land in which to live.

(right) Guelph; Church of Our Lady of the Immaculate Conception (1877–1926).

Old mill near Guelph.

University of Guelph.

University of Guelph.

Col. John McCrae's House, Guelph.

University of Guelph.

Oktoberfest Parade in Waterloo.

Ontario Highland Games at Fergus

Doon Pioneer Village.

'Woodside', Mackenzie King's boyhood home, Kitchener.

Aerial view of Fergus with
the Grand River.

Mennonite farm.

Mennonite mornings near St. Jacobs.

Rockwood Provincial Park.

(right) Mennonite ploughteam near St. Jacobs.

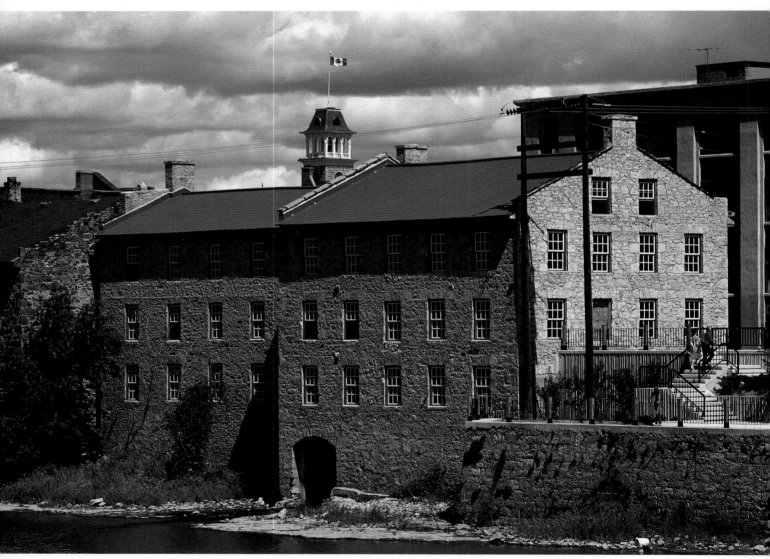

Cambridge along the Grand River.

Misty morning at New Hamburg.

The Conestogo River winds through Waterloo County.

Aerial view of Cambridge.

'Springbank Snow Countess', Woodstock.

Opera House, St. Mary's.

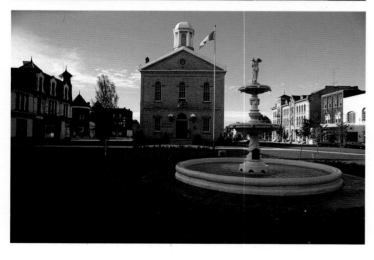

Old Town Hall (1852), Woodstock.

Farm at Shakespeare.

Festival Park, Stratford.

Dawn in the Festival Park, Stratford.

Stratford with a glimpse of the City Hall.

'The Old Prune' restaurant, Stratford.

Festival Theatre, Stratford.

'The Church' restaurant, Stratford.

Festival Theatre, Stratford.

Aerial view of 'The Square', Goderich.

Old CPR Station, Goderich.

Eldon House (1834), the oldest remaining house in London.

Fanshawe Pioneer Village, London.

Labatt's Pioneer Brewery, London.

Eldon House interior, London.

Interior, Regional Art Gallery, London.

Regional Art Gallery, London.

Urban renewal, London.

University of Western Ontario, London.

St. Paul's Anglican Cathedral (1846), London.

Attawanda Longhouse, University of Western Ontario.

Huron College, University of Western Ontario

University College,
University of Western
Ontario.

Cyclists in the fall, University of Western Ontario.

Brescia College, University of Western Ontario.

Freighter laid up for winter
in the St. Clair River,
Sarnia.

Country road near Sarnia.

Farmers' market, Dorchester.

Bluewater International Bridge, linking Sarnia with
Port Huron, Michigan.

Tecumseh's boulder, relic of the War of 1812, Fort Malden, Amherstburg.

Essex County farmland.

The Ambassador Bridge, linking Windsor to Detroit.

University of Windsor.

Spirit of Windsor, a 1911 CN locomotive, with Detroit across
the water.

Leamington, Lake Erie.

Dawn at Point Pelee.

Nature walk through Point Pelee National Park.

Uncle Tom's Cabin
Museum, Dresden.

Interior, Uncle Tom's Cabin Museum.

Grave of the Rev. Josiah Henson (1789–1883), founder of the American Institute for fugitive slaves.

Chapel, Uncle Tom's Cabin Museum.

TO BE SOLD,

A BLACK WOMAN, named PEGGY, aged about forty years ; and a Black boy her ſon, named JUPITER, aged about fifteen years, both of them the property of the Subſcriber.

The Woman is a tolerable Cook and waſher woman and perfectly underſtands making Soap and Candles.

The Boy is tall and ſtrong of his age, and has been employed in Country buſineſs, but brought up principally as a Houſe Servant—They are each of them Servants for life. The Price for the Wowan is one hundred and fifty Dollars—for the Boy two hundred Dollars, payable in three years with Intereſt from the day of Sale and to be properly ſecured by Bond &c.— But one fourth leſs will be taken in ready Money.

PETER RUSSELL.

Press cutting, Uncle Tom's Cabin Museum.

Main street of Paris.

(right) Brant's Ford, a stone in commemoration of the Mohawk chief Joseph Brant loyalist who gave his name to Brantford.

THIS BOULDER
MARKS THE SITE OF
BRANTS FORD
ERECTED BY THE
BRANT
HISTORICAL SOCIETY

Port Stanley, Lake Erie.

Port Burwell, Lake Erie.

Tobacco farm near Simcoe.

Tobacco farm near Delhi.

Port Dover, Lake Erie.

Simcoe town park.

Aerial view of Brantford.

(right) Mennonite sundown.

Dawn in Southwestern Ontario.